TURN KEY

A SCREENPLAY #X

JOHN E. WORDSLINGER

TURN KEY
a screenplay #X
by John E. WordSlinger

A SCREENPLAY NOT INTENDED AS AN ACCURATE PORTRAYAL OF REAL PEOPLE OR EVENTS

ISBN# 9798605252467

TURN KEY © 2019
by John E. WordSlinger/John E. O'Hara
johnewordslinger.wordpress.com
More Books Available @ amazon.com & lulu.com

Published PoetryTrain.com
& John E. WordSlinger
9840 S. Pulaski Rd. #101
Oaklawn, IL 60456

TURN KEY

A corrupted town 'Coltsville, Illinois, U.S.A. involved in illegal teeth commodity trading, and silence is the only way to stay alive.

THE BEGINING

EXT. NIGHT - COLTSVILLE

VIGILANTE, a tall person who wore all black, with a black cloth face
mask, carried a long gun, and a skinny sword set the opium house on
fire, and stood out front of this den.

As the house was burning, a man jumps out of second story window, and
many men run out the front door, and away. While inside, two tried to
go out the back door, but it was barricaded, and they were burned
alive inside.

                          VIGILANTE
                 You lawman opium smuggler,

                (White man of the law walks out.)

          I want you first. I am here to stop your fandango.

                (Shoots the man in the throat.)

TWO CHINA MEN run out, and charge the Vigilante, they engage in
martial arts, and the Vigilante slices one in the leg with his sword,
he turns, and shoots the other one in the leg. Another one runs out
of the house, runs at the Vigilante, and the Vigilante shots him in
the leg too. The three China men crawl on the ground, and one cries
in agony.

                          VIGILANTE
                 Stop your caterwauling!

    (Hits one China man in the head with the butt of his rifle, and it
    kills the man. He looks at another, shoots him twice, and he dies.
  The other one gets up, and limps away. The Vigilante walks fast, and
     faster up behind the China man, and slices him in the back of the
               arm, knocking him back to the ground.)

    No more happy happy paradise here in Coltsville for you, and your
                           Chinafalutin.

              (Looks closer into the China mans face.)

          Spread the word. Death-man will cut you down.

    (Turns around, looks at the burning house, walks to his horse, gets
                      on, and rides away.)

POV
Burning house.

FADE IN
EXT. DAY - TOWN OF COLTSVILLE

A boy delivers newspapers in town, and gives one to BARBER LEWIS
KELLS at the barber shop, and it reads.

    OPIUM DEN BURNS TO THE GROUND & 4 DEAD OUTSIDE & 2 INSIDE.

FADE OUT
EXT. DAY - DIRT ROAD

POV&S
Apples trees everywhere. Windmills turning and birds chirping.

MATT HEMINGS, a mix breed, with auburn hair, and hazel eyes. He be
Irish and American Native, although a red, white and blue just do the
right dang thing will you kind of man, and he's a Great Spirit
fearing man. People seemed to be afraid of his intelligence, the way
he carries himself they'd say. He's a book and dirt road smart
person, of course, he's a Wappelo-Hillbilly, and a new dam Yankee.

                    MATT HEMINGS
    (Lifted his head, the scents of the town came in his nostrils.)

                    V.O.
As I ride into this farm and horse town I do not have a good feeling
 in this sense of a new nation this country calls, the era of good
 feeling. What does newspaper editors know? Shot in the ankle three
years ago in the state of Indiana. I was near a shoot out I was not
 involved in. Now I am gimp, a man with a limp. A land pirate like,
  but all I pyrate, be time, before time pyrates me. Roofing was my
trade, and always a writer. Now writing be my profession. I carry not
  a gun although I should, to protect my intellectual property.

(A man rode by, as MATT pulled slightly out his brass knuckles.)

                    MATT HEMINGS
                    Howdy.

                    MAN ON HORSE
                    Howdy.

                              V.O.
I know not to look back, this be a trust thing, but do I trust this
person, furthermore does this person trust me? Has he turned around.
   I have learned not many folk know how to ride, or control their
                              horses.

                            (Laughs)

                          MAN ON HORSE
                (Turns around to look at MATT.)

Young boys play knock knock ditch.

                          MATT HEMINGS
                           (Smiles)

   I admit I am a lonely man, most of us men are. Literature keeps me
  keen, and mentally lean. Once I settle today I will start to read my
        new book I bought, 'The Sketch Book' by Geoffrey Crayon.

A Wells Fargo U.S. Mail wagon was ahead, and the driver had his hat
over his face nappin' as a woman, and a man walked by. The flapping
of the new thirteen stars and stripes United States flag caught MATTS
attention as he rode by, and he whistled the Star Spangled Banner
Song.

A small wagon train crossed paths with MATT, wagons of tobacco and
rice...

                            MATT
                  Mayhaps, the towns lute.

                            V.O.
  Everything in this town is fairly new, as I ride upon its square it
   looks as though the town has a new library, post office, theater,
            train station, and a new hospital being built.

Electricians were installing street lamps on the sidewalks.

MATT HEMINGS looked at the carpenters as they worked the hospital,
and seemingly the man in charge noticed MATT, and this man stared at
him as he rode by. The man's ASHER TOWNS, local contractor and
lawyer. A solid man, clean cut, blue stern eyes, a glimpse of him you
could tell, the man mastered the measuring stick, and a master of
tools. As MATT looked at him, ASHER combed his mustache with his
fingers, and then one knew, ASHER knew mankind, and mans laws.

Black men with bulls pulled wagons of sugar bags. One man shoved off a bag, a construction worker grabbed it up, and took it to the back of the construction zone.

The bank and the barbershop were next to each other. The blacksmith and the hotel were next to each other, and an ease set inside MATT.

                         MATT HEMINGS
          A bath from this unbearable dirt. Food and drink.

           (Looked back at the Barbershop, and read the signs.

             Sign read- CASH & TOBACCO FOR TEETH
   "Relief Administered, Consultations Free. No Cheap John Work Here."

                         MATT HEMINGS
       Dumb asses don't realize the tobacco be doing this to them.

FADE IN
INT. DAY - BARBERSHOP

A woman sits in a chair, and the BARBER LEWIS KELLS, a tall man, with a long face, and pouchy lips, furthermore his hair be red, bushy on the sides, and at top, his hair recedes, and his brown eyes were unlike any other person with brown eyes.

                       BARBER LEWIS KELLS
   Don't you worry, Mrs. Greenwood this won't hurt a bit, and if it
   does, well, I'll just shoot you, and we'll call it even. Now open
   wide. Bet, you look at apples different now. (Laughs) What, do you
                      not want to be tough?

MRS. ELIZABETH GREENWOOD was THOMAS GREENWOODS wife, and he be the
   towns banker. The U.S.A. Banking officer. She be beautiful, with
brown eyes and hair, that was always kept up, and pinned back. She be
a trivia type of lady, everything touched her. She be an apple lady,
              and an apple snapped a part of her tooth off.

                   MRS. ELIZABETH GREENWOOD
                    Yea imagine the future!

          (She looks at his ham-fisted dirty hands.)

                       BARBER LEWIS KELLS
   I know your families history. Oh slouch if you want to. We are going
   to say a prayer, and both of us are gonna have some alcohol with
                         opium in it.

(Farts)

Farmer Peabodys funky chickens.

(Pulls up the apron around her.)

There are no parks around here to walk in. This town wants spark, their smiling spark. This town wants to be controversy, unveiling their teeth. Beauty from durn ugly. People come from miles and miles to be here. People want to grin, they want to afford their own grin, and I smelt it all. Bad breath, good breath. Some have nasty words. I tell them, there are no whales, walrus or hippos around here. If you don't like what we have here then mail order your teeth from England. To be blessed but also venomous perhaps, against tooth worms. Okay drink some of this, and I'll dab your gums with magic water. So you have a mean rattler in your mouth. Soreness.

MRS. GREENWOOD
uh hu
(She threw the apple she brought with her, and clinched on.)

BARBER LEWIS KELLS
We have a pole, tough string, and pitch fork out there. I can tie your tooth to the pole, and jab you in the face with a pitchfork, your choice?

(He stalls, tilts his head, and smiles at her.)

Toothaches are everywhere like dust, them sawdust folk. Eye for an eye, tooth for a tooth. I need my beer foam towel. Going to pull, not file, and later a new tooth.

FADE OUT
EXT. DAY - OUTSIDE KINGERYS BROTHEL & PEARL HOTEL

Sheriff PAUL WALLACE, deputies, and local DR. ZANE SHULE rode fast up the road to Coltsvilles brothel, jumped off their horses, and ran into the brothel.

MATT HEMINGS
(Walked up the stairs of the hotel, many folk and keepers were on the porch.)

What happened?

                          HOTEL CLERK MR. PEARL
Mass suicide by laudanum. The oil of gladness in the era of gladness,
my ass, and I bet Miss big titted, I can hold up your coffee cups
                       maybe the one that induced this.

                             MATT HEMINGS
                        (Looked back at the brothel.)

                  Is there a book store in Coltsville?

                          HOTEL CLERK MR. PEARL
                               (Pointed)

         The general store. Two roads west, one road north.

A blonde with blue silverish eyes walked out the door of the hotel,
and MATT HEMINGS heart began to beat faster. CHRISTINA BURZ, her hair
braided beautifully like no other, with two rolls rolling back down
the middle, way past her shoulder, and the sides of her hair be
tightly pulled to the two rolls on each side. Her dress stopped
above, covering her breasts and that was as high as the top of the
dress went. Exposing her smooth skin, shoulders, and her luring neck.

CHRISTINA BURZ walked on by without a glance at MATT. The HOTEL CLERK
MR. PEARL looked at her, at MATT, at her again, and MATT walked near
the door.

                          HOTEL CLERK MR. PEARL
                  Come in. Welcome to the Pearl.

                             MATT HEMINGS
                               (Followed.)
                           Impressive Sir.

FADE OUT
INT. DAY - BLACKSMITH SHOP

Sign said, LOCKWOODS PLOWS, HORSE SHOEING, HARROWS, MACHINE REPAIR &
TOOTH REMOVAL

CAM PAN IN THROUGH

BLACK SMITH FRANK LOCKWOOD, a blacksmith. He be a tall handsome man,
with long dark hair, blue eyes, and a mustache that tops a smile that
makes everyones day for them.

                    BLACK SMITH FRANK LOCKWOOD
                         (Making chains)

ELSY WHEELER, a seamstress. She be tall, with short dark hair, and
deep dark eyes, furthermore held a stern beauty.

                          ELSY WHEELER
A shipment of horse feed arrived, and the Deere and Company are here
     too, with the steel plow, and hay forks needs repair.

                    BLACK SMITH FRANK LOCKWOOD
Elsy the church bells are done, and chains will be done here in a
                             scorch.

                          ELSY WHEELER
I am a sure you heard. PRAIRIE MARY DIVIN has not stopped sobbing
          since the news reached her this morning.

                    BLACK SMITH FRANK LOCKWOOD
That's what happens when you dance with the devil. This town's trying
   to turn it into a gold fork. New equipment from Scotland should be
                         here next week.

                          ELSY WHEELER
You are way to busy, and going to have to hire someone soon.

                    BLACK SMITH FRANK LOCKWOOD
I may hire that French Lytton boy. Every time he is here with his
     father he touches everything, and he did ask for work.

                          ELSY WHEELER
Teach him to be mightier than the sword like you Frank.

                    BLACK SMITH FRANK LOCKWOOD
                           (Laughs)
Strong willed. I am no Poet. I am sure the gutter press will kill the
                       brothel tomorrow.

FADE IN
EXT. DAY - CEMETERY

Coltsvilles' sexton undertaker REX 'SPLINTER' WATERS wheel checked
his horse drawn hearse, and next to it were fleets of hearse wagons,
and a few jail wagons.

REX 'SPLINTER' WATERS, a short haired, clean shaven man. His stare
was always the same, one brow up, that eye was his spear eye, and the
other brow and eye was clearly looking directly to you, waiting for
your defense. Seemed scary was fun to him.

                        REX 'SPLINTER' WATERS
No more burying on the spot. Prompt service they want, prompt service
                              they get.

                       GROUP OF UNDERTAKERS
           (Walked horses to the hearses, and one spoke.)

         Ol Father Hubbard, more bones for the bone yard.

                        REX 'SPLINTER' WATERS
             We seek no ghosts, we seek what ghosts leave.

(Looks at his pocket watch, boarded his hearse wagon, rode into town,
                 and his undertaker crew followed.)

FADE IN
INT. DUSK - HOTEL (Upstairs)

                           MATT HEMINGS
(Cleaned Up. He looked out the window, observed everyone, and wrote.)

POV -as he wrote
On the Saloon deck Saloon girls danced and sang, lured the people of
Coltsville inside to drink and gamble. The towns untamed were all
about. Street musicians jammed, and drunkards staggered.

                              V.O.
   They are doing what they know best, live as if it were their last
day. To do what they will do in time, their time and time again. This
                     was the American Frontier.

 Seems no one thought of tribal Chiefs, or Holy men of any men. They
      were celebrating Florida, Florida was theirs now. They were
   manifesting, pushing, making the west wild. This America was a
 toddler to other nations. Law and order were breaking down as it were
         being ordered up. Tensions were everywhere.

 This town's on life fire, and the pastures around the town filled
with cattle were also filled with fox fires. The grass and horn tips
               glowed. What a beautiful site.

                (MATT underlined that in his journal as he wrote)
        <u>(The grass and horn tips glowed. What a beautiful site. St. Elmos
                                  fires.)</u>

FADE OUT
EXT. DAWN - OUTSIDE KINGERY BROTHEL

DR. ZANE SHULE, a scary looking man, walks out of the brothel, and
SHERIFF PAUL WALLACE, an even more scary looking man, followed him,
and shoots some bullets into the air. His deputies drag out the
suicide corpses into the middle of the street.

                         SHERIFF PAUL WALLACE
      (Turns in a circle as a crowd watches him, shoots one more time.)

                       Extra-judicial punishment!

FADE IN
INT. DAWN - HOTEL ROOM

The outside ruckus awakes MATT.

                            MATT HEMINGS
   (Looks out the window, and sees the lawmen ride away. Townsfolk walk
      up to all the bodies, and some bend over to get a closer look.)

          REX 'SPLINTER' WATERS & HIS GROUP OF UNDERTAKERS
                     (Load the bodies into wagons.)

                           CHRISTINA BURZ
         (Rode her horse into the direction of the bookstore.)

                            MATT HEMINGS
     I realize here I am in great peril. Groups of this, and gangs of
                                that.

Cow pokes rode by with twenty plus cattle. There was a knock on MATTS
room door.

HOTEL MAID, a beautiful Spanish woman, curvy and short.

                             HOTEL MAID
    Mr. Hemings I brought you your breakfast, and will be bringing you
   hot water into the bathing room. Here are your brushes you asked for
                   and your newspaper. Extra candles too.

                              MATT HEMINGS
Thank you. I have a complaint. Walls are to thin, and seems to me,
ignorance be thick. Slamming doors, and playing music in late hours.

                              HOTEL MAID
                              (Laughs)

              I will tell LEROY, the HOTEL CLERK MR. PEARL.

                              MATT HEMINGS
Be there a print shop in town? Does Coltsville have a publisher?

                              HOTEL MAID
         Yes, the Chinese run one on the end of Main street.

                              MATT HEMINGS
              Thank you, food looks and smells grand.

                              HOTEL MAID
                              (Smiles.)

          I will return when tub is full of hot lilac water.

                              MATT HEMINGS
                              Lilac water?

FADE IN
POVS
Dogs were barking and children we heard outside. Poor folk walked in
front of a covered wagon. The ground was vibrating, a locomotive
train could be heard.

FADE BACK

                              HOTEL MAID
                              (Smiles.)

   Yes, you want the ladies don't you. I think, hmm, Brackenridge &
   Fowler, but I am not sure where, maybe east of town. They run the
   local art gallery and theater down by Bear River. Follow the crick
                          behind the hotel.

                              MATT HEMINGS
The west wouldn't exist without women like you. What be your name?

                           HOTEL MAID
                           (Smiles)

         MARCIA ROBBINS. You smell good, not like Mountain Men.

                           MATT HEMINGS
                           (Laughed.)

Happy to know there be no lice and seam squirrels, furthermore other
                              bugs.

                           HOTEL MAID
                  We take heart in this place Mr. Hemings.

FADE OUT
INT. DAY - LOCKWOODS BLACKSMITH SHOP

                    BLACK SMITH FRANK LOCKWOOD
          (Taking out a maleruption tooth of a sedated horse.)

You have a pack of wolf teeth in there young girl. No biting, because
          the upper tooth must go first. Going to go slow.

                        BARBER LEWIS KELLS
   (Walks into the shop, shoots a bullet at the bell, and it ricochets.
                   Scaring FRANK and the horse.)

                    BLACK SMITH FRANK LOCKWOOD
           (Grabs a knife from the ground, and darts towards LEWIS.)

                       SHERIFF PAUL WALLACE
           (Walks in with his gun out, and points it at FRANK.)

The bell for the Hospital Church the People call, and to the grave it
   summons all. For now on animals be your only means of dentistry. I
          will write a letter to the Revere Company also FRANK.

                    ELSY WHEELER & the LYTTON BOY
              (Walk in the shop, and she looks at everyone.)

Sheriff don't you have bootleggers to harass. There are trails all
    over my cattle ranch. I have been thinking, thinking to be a
          Detective of this county. Not private if needed.

                       SHERIFF PAUL WALLACE
                    (Looked at her pistol.)

                              ELSY WHEELER
I am not bluffing. I hear the affairs from mouths, and they want a
                                 feeding.

                          SHERIFF PAUL WALLACE
                      (Looked at LEWIS, and FRANK.)

                      I meant what I said Frank.

        (He walked out looking at Elsy, and Lewis followed.)

                              ELSY WHEELER
              I don't sleep much. I rest speaking my mind.

                        BLACK SMITH FRANK LOCKWOOD
                   You are going to get yourself killed.

                              ELSY WHEELER
You think I am alone. We have PRAIRIE MARY DIVIN. All will be cozy.
              She's a fortune teller you know.

FADE OUT
INT. DAY - HOTEL BATH ROOM

                              MATT HEMINGS
          Here's two dollars. Must have soap. Keep the change.

                       HOTEL MAID MARCIA ROBBINS
                                (Smiles)

Thank you, you are not like these dudes around here. I will have
      newspaper for you every morning. Ready to shave you.

                              MATT HEMINGS
(Undresses, climbs in the tub, and reads his paper as Marcia mixed
                             the lather.)

                  Thanks, never will be either.

(PAPER READ: 4 found Dead on Greenbrier Road. Was it an act of
Vigilance? The town must ask, Did the Vigilante strike KINGERYS
            BROTHEL Or did 6 Women Commit Suicide?)

                       HOTEL MAID MARCIA ROBBINS
          Some people here are very bad. Be careful here.

                              MATT HEMINGS
                       I am with the do-gooders.

FADE OUT
EXT. DAY - CHURCH CEMETERY

            PREACHER DUNN, short & Stocky, full of grace

        You have been busy since Christmas Day of last year.

                          REX 'SPLINTER' WATERS
        Been busy since I was a boy. I still use my great grand daddys'
        lantern and shovel. Not no community thing you know, round here.

                             PREACHER DUNN
                    I'll be ringing the bell for you.

                          REX 'SPLINTER' WATERS
        I don't look over my shoulder Preacher Dunn. I get the job done. My
        hands carried every stone, most dug by hand, and stacked over yonder
        by the barn. My back stack. My mausoleum material. I know human
        mortality more than you. I also unearthed every unmarked grave on
                             this property.

                             PREACHER DUNN
                  What are you thoughts about these gals?

                          REX 'SPLINTER' WATERS
        I knew them all, and they knew me. All I can say. When you are a
        sinner, you are a sinner. We are going to need a train load of
                       charcoal. Winter's coming.

                             PREACHER DUNN
                 Rex, you can break sin, like you break frost.

                          REX 'SPLINTER' WATERS
                             Is that so?

                             PREACHER DUNN
                   (Looked at him, and walked away.)

FADE IN
EXT. DAY - HOSPITAL ROOF TOP

                              ASHER TOWN
        We have no yellow fever here as of yet, only God fever, passerbys.

BANKER THOMAS GREENWOOD, a typical greedy bastard, with that I can take out a bank robber look.

And those we should treat with royalty so they return, strikingly luckily.

ASHER TOWN
I understand.

BANKER THOMAS GREENWOOD
A new batch of Taveau silver mixed with mercury came in on the train.

ASHER TOWN
This is not a population of great thinkers.

BANKER THOMAS GREENWOOD
I have to meet with farmer CLAY PEABODY later today. Come to the bank at noon, and I'll pay you another third.

ASHER TOWN
I won't let any of this crack. Thanks for this chain transaction, this delivery cycle will be concealed.

BANKER THOMAS GREENWOOD
Asher get with Jackson, a revenge is at hand. He will be sweeping the nation. We will be rewarded. You use TnT, and I also use TnB; threats and bribery.

FADE OUT
EXT. DAY - FORTUNE TELLER HOME

PRAIRIE MARY DIVIN, beautiful in every way, sandy blonde hair, and blue eyes. She was a master at accents.

PRAIRIE MARY DIVIN
Deputy why do you congregate on the side of my home, and when someone rides by you getty up, and go? You are wasting tax payers money. If you want to spend some money wisely come inside, and let me the Coltsville gypsy tell you about fortunes from my lipsy.

(Winks.)

I will be gentle as golden dreams.

                         DEPUTY
                  (Walks up to MARY.)

You have my interest. I like overflowing gold coins. I like unseen
                       knowledge.

                   PRAIRIE MARY DIVIN
            (Touches his collar, and smiles.)

                         DEPUTY
                   You are always busy.

                   PRAIRIE MARY DIVIN
Yes, and something tells me. I won't know how to say stop with you.

FADE OUT
INT. DAY - GENERAL STORE

                      MATT HEMINGS
I want to telegraph Chicago. Do you also do heliographic
              communication, and smoke signals.

                      MR. TEMPLE,
a big man, & SON-BYRON, a younger version of his father
                       (Laughs.)

               Write out your message sir.

                      MATT HEMINGS
         Thanks. Interested in your books, and ink.

                   MR. TEMPLE & SON
             You a geographer or surveyor?

                      MATT HEMINGS
Yes, but for the funny papers. Hope of salvation. Literary historian.
          Down to earth though, how I was weaned.

                   TEMPLES SON BYRON
I will show you where the books are. We have a book room. New
shipment will come by train next week. New books we have are, David
Thomas, Travels Through the Western Country Ohio Indiana Map West
Frontier. Memoirs, of John Evelyn, John Watkins, and James Caulfield.

                     CHRISTINA BURZ
          (Sat in the book room reading a book.)

MATT HEMINGS
(His heart began to beat faster.)

CHRISTINA BURZ
(Looked over her book of English fashion, and eye flirted with Matt.)

TEMPLES SON BYRON
I will bring you coffee on us, since you are new, and write out your
telegraph to Chicago sir?
(Looks at Matt questioning his name.)

MATT HEMINGS
Matt Hemings.

TEMPLES SON BYRON
Byron.

CHRISTINA BURZ
This country going to panic over nickles and dimes. They're fighting
over Goldie Locks, not know that is me.

(Laughs)

I do like sharp loans. Are you a farmer Mr. Hemings?

MATT HEMINGS
A rugged writer, and historian.

CHRISTINA BURZ
Farmers here are finding their land rising, unlike other areas,
dropping. Can I sit with you, I liked to be spun like a mill.
MATT HEMINGS
(Writing his message.)

Yes, feel comfortable.

CHRISTINA BURZ
A bottle of Pine Top whiskey would do that. Liquid infrastructure.

MATT HEMINGS
(Laughs, and his heart beat began to beat faster.)

CHRISTINA BURZ
I am a federal power historian of sorts.
(Laughs.)

Share of the spoils.

MR. TEMPLE
(Takes MATTS message, and brings whiskey.)

CHRISTINA BURZ
You seem to be looking for honey, and as well as some bear to save you.

MATT HEMINGS
(Laughs)

CHRISTINA BURZ
You have a room at the Pearl. Let's go there.

MATT HEMINGS
No need to persist. I have dissolved.

CHRISTINA BURZ
I am a fire the oceans waters can not put out. I am a Virginian. I know what I want.

MR. TEMPLE
(Listens and watches them.)

V.O.
Only the seas of blood.

ELSY WHEELER came in the store, as MATT gives MR. TEMPLE money and his message. CHRISTRINA, and him leave.

ELSY WHEELER
Mr. Temple who is that man with her?

MR. TEMPLE
Seems law biding. Mr. Matt Hemings.

ELSY WHEELER
I have a message to Washington D.C. Kansas are like us, about ready to kill the banks.

MR. TEMPLE
We are like the three monkeys, see, hear, and speak no evil. Farmers have lowered their prices with me, but I have to raise my prices to float.

ELSY WHEELER
Our secret, we will kill the bank.

FADE IN
INT. DAY - BARBER SHOP

                        BARBER LEWIS KELLS
                        (Reading the newspaper.)

                        REX 'SPLINTER' WATERS
                    (Walks in, and hands him teeth.)
     Nearly six sets. Most are good, and I am not concerned about the
    prices of cotton and grain. I like folly, this is how I make money.
      Putting bodies in the ground, and their teeth in your hands. The
    countries music has stopped playing, except for here. Acres, gold and
       silver, and everyone here going to get you rich, and me richer.

                        BARBER LEWIS KELLS
                Going to be a painful hangover for most.

                        REX 'SPLINTER' WATERS
                Grass of the grasshopper Lewis.

                        BARBER LEWIS KELLS
                        (Laughs)

    That's good, real good. What's also good, is, political drunkards who
       cut their teeth watching statesmen sit side by side and politely
     debate the issues of the time. Economic fault lines have opened, and
     cracked teeth, and cracked mirrors are going to make us rich. We have
                            to stay small.

                        REX 'SPLINTER' WATERS
       Nine million people in the U.S.A., and many are born and die
     everyday. This depression will rhyme, and we are going to have to be
                            on time.

                        BARBER LEWIS KELLS
                        (Laughs)

       I love a crisis. Teeth and cash circulation. Legit goods.

                        REX 'SPLINTER' WATERS
                Better than a book or a play.

    A slight tremor was felt, shaking up the town.

                        REX 'SPLINTER' WATERS
        That there, if nay stronger would stir the crop and pot.
                        (Laughs)

                    BARBER LEWIS KELLS
                (Hands REX a bag of gold.)

                    What about jewelry?

                    REX 'SPLINTER' WATERS
                You know where to find me.

FADE OUT
EXT. DAY - COLTSVILLE

CHRISTINA BURZ & MATT HEMINGS walked to the hotel. She noticed Matts
limp.

                    MATT HEMINGS
    Did you know most spouses cheat on their spouses during war time?

                    CHRISTINA BURZ
Yes, I went to church. Do you go to church? Why did you ask me that?

                    MATT HEMINGS
                Seems no one be loyal.

                    CHRISTINA BURZ
Wood and lumber is where the work is at here in Coltsville, and real
                        estate.

                    MATT HEMINGS
                Power or liberty?

                    CHRISTINA BURZ
                Great question.

                    MATT HEMINGS
            What do you do for a living?

                    CHRISTINA BURZ
    If I told you, I'd have to kill you. Allies are allies, on a even
            keel, and a mutual spirit. All I can say.

A crazy tall black man ran up to them, and tackled Matt to the
ground.
                    MATT HEMINGS
            Let me up, and what are you doing?

                          BLACK MAN
                    (Looked at Matt good.)

        I am sorry I thought you were someone else.

                        MATT HEMINGS
(Got up, and the man walked away, so they walked on. Three lawmen
seen this ordeal, and rode up to them with their fire arms pointing
                          at Matt.)

                          LAWMAN
                Why did you assault that man?

                        MATT HEMINGS
                I did not. He assaulted me.

                          LAWMAN
(Got closer to MATT, very close. As so did the other two lawmen,
               aiming their guns at MATT.)

                        MATT HEMINGS
(Keeled over in a martial arts stance, and was about to take the
                      lawmans' rifle.)

          I can make this green grass sticky red!

                    SHERIFF PAUL WALLACE
              (Rode up to the confrontation.)

Arms down. He means it, back down. He is un-armed. What is your name,
   and why are you here in Coltsville? Where are you two going?

                        MATT HEMINGS
Matt Hemings, and yesterday I moved here to live. To dine, and then
                       my hotel room.

                    SHERIFF PAUL WALLACE
Be on your way, and you LESTER, get back home.

                  (Black man walked home.)

                        MATT HEMINGS
                Do you know that man?

                          CHRISTINA BURZ
Perhaps, he's on drugs, and a foot soldier for local dealers.

          (Drinks some whiskey, and passes it to MATT.)

                          MATT HEMINGS
                          (Drinks.)

      What do you think the future's going to be like?

                          CHRISTINA BURZ
Hopefully not a lot of horse shit. People here don't want to improve
        themselves, and our country is all about that.

When they came upon the hotel, a man was on the stairs playing a
wooden flute.

          DR. PIERRE SAPPINGTON, a sharp dressed man.
      (Starred at Christinas' chest as he talked to her.)

You two look as though you are enjoying the day. Let me get out of
                          your way.

                          (Gets up.)

I am the knew Doctor in town, and will be running the new hospital
                      with Dr. Shules.

                          CHRISTINA BURZ
                        Thank you Sir.

                          MATT HEMINGS
Matt Hemings, and this be Christina Burz. I am a writer, and she is a
                          mystery.

                        (Shook hands.)

                    DR. PIERRE SAPPINGTON
                          (Laughs)

Beauty is a mystery. I love music, and Greek Poetry. I also love
killing fevers, except love fever, so let me move on, and you two can
                        carry on.

                          MATT HEMINGS
                          (Laughs.)

                        CHRISTINA BURZ
                    Welcome to Coltsville.

                      PIERRE SAPPINGTON
        Thank you Madam, nice place for a young physician to start.

                        CHRISTINA BURZ
                          (Smiles.)

        Doctor Sappington this town is growing, and your hands and time's
                          going to be full.

                      DR.PIERRE SAPPINGTON
                 That's why they hired me darling.

                   (Walks away playing his flute.)

                        CHRISTINA BURZ
        I go to the Omaha lodge for the medicine woman, smoke great medicine,
          and sing chants. Look the Kingery brothel is back in business.

        Railroaders red lighten lanterns were on the porch of the brothel.

                         MATT HEMINGS
                 Let's go inside the Hotel room.

                             V.O.
        I should go about this a different way. I like this woman a lot. I
                  don't want to drink. It's my flaw.

FADE OUT
EXT. DAY - CHURCH TOWER

                    BLACK SMITH FRANK LOCKWOOD
        Last of the ten bells, and the smallest one. They call it a curfew
                              bell.

                        PREACHER DUNN
                    We are going to need it.

                    BLACK SMITH FRANK LOCKWOOD
        I brought extra wheels, stays and sliders. Let's go to the chiming
             apparatus, and teach each other to peal the bells.

FADE OUT
EXT. DAY - COLTSVILLE

The new church bells sound away, nearly everyone in town and around
hear the bells, most come outside the hear better.

FADE TO & FRO & TO

                         MR. TEMPLE and BYRON
 Creme de la crème. She really does have her own unique and beautiful
tone. Sing the bells, bells, bells, bells Bells, bells, bells, bells.

                         PRAIRIE MARY DIVIN
Either enemy is attacking or it is warding off the enemy. Not the
           Bells of Notre-Dame de Paris, good enough though.

                           NEWSPAPER MAN
                    (Taking notes and photographs.)

            REX 'SPLINTER' WATERS & GROUP OF UNDERTAKERS
                 (Stop digging graves to hear the bells.)

         THE GREENWOODS, DR. ZANE SHULE & ASHER TOWN
               (Step outside the bank to hear the bells.)

                         BARBER LEWIS KELLS
                 (Looks out of the barber shop window.)

                             THE BELLS
               Awake Coltsville, hauntingly beautiful.

                         MATT & CHRISTRINA
                      (Open the hotel window.)

                           MATT HEMINGS
                      You sure are a looker.

                          CHRISTINA BURZ
                        Prime cut honey.

FADE OUT
EXT. NIGHT - COLTSVILLE

An owl hooted, cattle rested, horses on watch, and wild camels walked
on the lands of Coltsville.

FADE IN
INT. NIGHT - JAIL CELL

                              MATT HEMINGS
                    (Awakes in a jail cell, confused.)

                                JAILER
Time to take a photograph. This way we know who you are, and reward
                   collecting if any one day.

                              MATT HEMINGS
                    What, what am I in here for?

                                JAILER
          Disturbing the peace, and harassing a deputy.

                              MATT HEMINGS
                                 What?

                                JAILER
      You were drunk. Claiming a woman stole your address book, and
demanding him to find it, and you passed out. I will be taking you to
                          see the judge later.

A photograph was taken, and the Jailer gave Matt a plate of food.

                              MATT HEMINGS
                            (Ate his food.)

SALVADOR, a big Hispanic with a star tattoo under his left eye.

                                SALVADOR
          Why are you in here? You look like a murderer.

                              MATT HEMINGS
                          Disturbing the peace.

                                SALVADOR
             Nice. What are you others in here for?

(Three other inmates, said they were in there over domestic charges.)

                                JAILER
    Anthony, and Salvador your turn to see the Judge, so turn around.

ANTHONY, a big half breed American Native and Irish man, more
threatening than Salvador once one looked closer at him.

ANTHONY
I have a back injury, so cuff me in the front.

JAILER
I can't do that.

ANTHONY
You will regret that.

SALVADOR
Asshole, once we get out of here, we are coming to your house for dinner.

ANTHONY
(Laughs)
And we are going to sue you, and this town.

SALVADOR
The Judge isn't going to like that, and the Judge going to fire you.

A black man prisoner looked at Anthony.

ANTHONY
Don't be looking at me hard nigger. I am not the one who makes you bail cotton. I don't have cotton for you.

BLACK MAN
Don't let me catch you out there bandito on a cattle drive. I will black wash you, and turn you into dog food.

JAILER
Shut up!

(Cuffs them both, and brings them to court.)

MATT HEMINGS
(Lays down, pondering what happened.)

FADE OUT
INT - DAY - BLACKSMITH SHOP
ELSY WHEELER
Frank I sent out information to Washington D.C., and an outside newspaper.

BLACK SMITH FRANK LOCKWOOD
Let's hope Mr. Temple is on our side.

                         ELSY WHEELER
                      You have me worried.

                  BLACK SMITH FRANK LOCKWOOD
          The world is full of horse shit artists Elsy.

                     (Kisses, and holds her.)

FADE IN
INT. DAY - JAIL
                           ANTHONY
    Cocaine. Oh ya, that stuff there, I put it on my best gun, and she
    was like a fish, doing them lips, sucking all of it up. Them gals
                            love it.

                           SALVADOR
      Yeah, any of you all need any, look for me in the Saloon.

                           ANTHONY
      When you find your address book, you should beat her down.

                           SALVADOR
    Hopefully her coochie wasn't fishy, hairy and tasted like pennies.

                           JAILER
                      Hemings, let's go!

The jailer cuffs Matt, and takes him to court.

                           JAILER
Those men are insane, and dangerous. Stay away from them. Do you hear
                            me?

                        MATT HEMINGS
(Matt looked up at the Jailer, because his voice changed a little but
                        different.)

                           Yes.

                           JAILER
    The judge will drop charges. Listen to me, drinking disturbs the
  thinking. You think you think well while under drink, but you don't.
  I deal with drunks everyday. Some woman are bad, stay away from them.

FADE IN
EXT. NIGHT - RAIL YARD

Two rabbits run out of the woods, and across the railway tracks.

                    ONE RAILROADER
        Two cars of lumber to Boston, one to Chicago.

Railway men were loading lumber on a train car, and one walked near
the wagons to where ANTHONY & SALVADOR were there making a drug deal
with one.

                       VIGILANTE
   (Comes silently and quick around wagon of lumber towards the two
  bandito drug dealers. The railroader sees the Vigilante, and has no
  time to warm the banditos. The Vigilante shoots the railroader in the
                          throat.)

   Curtains up. I am Mr. Harmony, a man of light. You can't foil me,
  you're classification now, is alive, alive in hell. Curtains down,
                        town worms.

  (With no time to defend themselves the Vigilante slices up ANTHONY &
       SALVADOR, and sneaks off into the darkness of the night.)

FADE OUT
INT. DAY - HOTEL

MATT HEMINGS as he walked in he over heard many conversations in the
thin walled hotel. Kill this person, beat up this one, rob this one
and people having sex, furthermore news of the Coltsville Vigilante
&c etc.

                 HOTEL MAID MARCIA ROBBINS
     Good Morning Mr. Hemings. I brought you breakfast, and your
    newspaper. Sorry to hear about your rough night. As I said, be
   careful. If you have to make a telegraph today, best do it early
  because the whole town will be there over banks going bankrupt, and
   calling in loans all over the nation. People are afraid they will
  loose their properties to foreclosure. Rumors are, the sheriff and
   other officials, with two principal creditors are appearing on
                       peoples door steps.

                       MATT HEMINGS
  Okay, and I am sure they will take all, except the clothes people
                        stand in.

                    HOTEL MAID MARCIA ROBBINS
        Good news is, the Vigilante came to Coltsville again.

                          MATT HEMINGS
                     (Opening the newspaper.)
                   I read, and thank you Marcia.

                        (Gives her a tip.)

   Oh Philadelphia, scientifick mudpuppies, and publick uneducated
vandals. I have to keep my head down, although up, and focus on my
leather stocking series. Time will bury you Hemmings if you are not
   clever. I must be distinguishable, a diamond in a dunghill.

                      (Spoke as he wrote.)

                            V.O.
   Our generation, and yours will be struck, and when will we accept
  what we bleed? All is not lost though, and even if it was? We, and
the next generation will have a good ride, and perhaps those who come
      after us will take a note and everyone is wiser for it.

Todays news, 14 people dead by the hand of the Vigilante, and he left
a note. I am coming for the four fangs of evil of this town.

 Oh yes, my telegraph request, and a horse shoe. Good omen, bad omen,
 only God knows, maybe God be the Vigilante? Oh yes, my address book?

Chaos could be heard in the Pearl hotel lobby. Matt opened his door,
and briefly listened.
                           PUPILS
 This place has no future. Why are you so suspicious? You are crazy.
The future is wheat, cotton, tobacco, and corn. We are people, and we
                are going to stay. You are stupid.

                          MATT HEMINGS
                  (Silently closes the door.)

FADE OUT
EXT. DAY - MAINS STREET - COLTSVILLE

MR & MRS. GREENWOOD the bankers of Coltsville were riding in a
stagecoach into town. The coach stopped in front of the bank, because
someone painted the word 'SHAME' on the banks front door.

                          ELIZABETH GREENWOOD
Thomas it looks as though you have a different kind of bad bad tooth.
   No vanity left, and you will struggle to regain clients' and
  regulators' trust. How many bars of gold have you offered your
                        wealthy clients Thomas?

                       BANKER THOMAS GREENWOOD
                   (He gets out of the stagecoach.)
            Go put a tooth in your mouth, that I paid for.

                          ELIZABETH GREENWOOD
Clean up your own messes. Always knew something stank in Coltsville.
 Have fun with the People of Coltsville, and hope the Federal Reserve
   don't come a storming into town. This town has been waking up to
    madness, and I am interested in your alibis. Drive driver.

Stage coach rides off to the Dentist/Barber appointment.

FADE IN
INT. DAY - GENERAL STORE

Mr. Temples' son Byron rung the cash register as fast as he could for
the people in line with merchandise. The town of Coltsville was in an
uproar. MR. TEMPLE working the telegraph as people inside the store
were talking loud, and he heard as he worked as fast as he could to
suffice.
                              PUPILS
What's going to happen to the sawmill? What's going to happen to the
 flour mill? Does this mean the railroad cafe will close? You are out
                          of gun powder!
                            Mr. TEMPLE
                         (Looks at Byron.)
                  Keep doing what you are doing?

In the back of the store ELSY WHEELER and PRAIRIE MARY DIVIN were
conversing.

                            ELSY WHEELER
            Who's the royalty of the card table here in town?

                         PRAIRIE MARY DIVIN
 I can find out for you. Did you know the children of Coltsville are
   putting coins on the grave stones of the Vigilante victims?
                            ELSY WHEELER
                              Why?

                    PRAIRIE MARY DIVIN
              So a curse doesn't come upon them.

                       ELSY WHEELER
    SHERIFF PAUL WALLACE can't find any evidence as I gather evidence
                          upon him.

                    PRAIRIE MARY DIVIN
        Maybe this person is good, our night watchman.

                       ELSY WHEELER
           What makes you think this person is a man?

                    PRAIRIE MARY DIVIN
                     Great question.

                       ELSY WHEELER
        I am going to add more strain to SHERIFF PAUL WALLACE.

                    PRAIRIE MARY DIVIN
    We are magnificent agents. Maybe this Vigilante is from a surrounding
                           town?

                       ELSY WHEELER
     The mayor of Coltsville is away on vacation in his own house.

    A crew of electricians were in the cafe section too, one spoke.

                       ELECTRICIAN
    Oh for John Henry. I will help with the telegraphs, this horseshit
           will delay the night light ceremony this weekend.

    MATT HEMINGS walks into the general store.

                          BYRON
                        (Smiles.)

    Good Morning Mr. Hemings, we have your book, The Life and Morals of
    Jesus of Nazareth, sent by Mr. Abler himself. Also a Chicago reply.

                       MATT HEMINGS
         Thank you. I need a horseshoe, and some Cactus wine.

                        MR. TEMPLE
    We have Cactus wine, but you can get a horseshoe from FRANK LOCKWOOD,
               at his shop at the end of main street.

                        MATT HEMINGS
                  Posterity for me today.

SHERIFF PAUL WALLACE, and the deputy that MATT had an incident with
walked into the store.

                     SHERIFF PAUL WALLACE
        Matt, we need to speak with you. Come outside with us.

Everyone in the store witnessed this. ELSY WHEELER and PRAIRIE MARY
DIVIN looked at each other, and raised their eyebrows. A Wells Fargo
U.S. mail wagon pulled up as they walked outside.

FADE OUT
INT. DAY - BARBERSHOP

                      BARBER LEWIS KELLS
    (Opens his shop, and the Vigilante was sitting in his barber chair.)

             I like your hat Sir. How can I help you?

                          VIGILANTE
      I let myself in, and I came to introduce you to a myth. I am a
      folklorist, and I want to tell you about a hole, and about fire,
    furthermore ravens and rodents are on their way. They came to me for
                              help.

(Gets up, and punches LEWIS KELLS in the mouth. He speaks as he drags
Lewis into a back room. In that back room, the floor boards have been
    pulled up, and a hole large enough for a body to lay in was dug.)

      Do you feel any wings yet? To many people have gave their last
      nickels. So now you are going to have to surrender your hoarded
    goods. An exchange for say, lifeblood. An exchange, a change. Do you
      feel inflation yet? Unlike good people, you won't turn into gold.
                Maybe I should be an enterprise, global.

BARBER LEWIS KELLS struggles as the Vigilante ties up Lewis, and
slings him in the hole. A hole filled with oil shale. The Vigilante
struck a match, threw it in the hole, and the fire began, burning the
clothes, and so on. The Vigilante walked out the door, and the shop
caught on fire.

                   MRS. ELIZABETH GREENWOOD
    (Walked towards the shop as the stagecoach road away.)

THE VIGILANTE
Madam, Mr Kells is being forced to be burned up with remorse as of
now. I would not go inside the shop.

MRS. ELIZABETH GREENWOOD
Who are you?

VIGILANTE
A good Samaritan. MRS. Greenwood, I would advise you to begin, a
chain of love mail.

MRS. ELIZABETH GREENWOOD runs away, as the Vigilante gets on his
horse, and rides away.

FADE IN
EXT. DAY - OUTSIDE THE GENERAL STORE

SHERIFF PAUL WALLACE and MATT HEMINGS walk, and a deputy follow.

SHERIFF PAUL WALLACE
I found your address book. Why are you here in Coltsville?

MATT HEMINGS
Thanks. To make a home, and write.

SHERIFF PAUL WALLACE
What do you write?

MATT HEMINGS
A little bit of everything. I do not write anonymously as many do. I
have nothing to hide. Hiding to me is ridiculous. I burn on my own
coals, and am not afraid to do so. I judge not others, so that my
spirit be free. Admiration Sir. Have you seen Miss Burz?

SHERIFF PAUL WALLACE
No I have not.

Another deputy rode up fast, and spoke.

DEPUTY
Paul the barber shop is in flames. Seems the Vigilante has struck in
daylight, and Mrs. Greenwood is in shock.

SHERIFF PAUL WALLACE
(Looks at Matt.)

I have no more questions.

(Looks at the other deputy, they get to their horses, and ride away.)

ELSY WHEELER & PRAIRIE MARIE has been watching this, they look at each other, and they leave the General Store. Matt returns in for his book, and cactus wine.

                              PUPIL
                   You are out of gun powder!

FADE OUT
EXT. DAY - FARM

COLTSVILLE FARMER WILLIAM CALL, a family man, stern and strong, walks into his farm house.

                          WILLIAM CALL
James Monroe is the problem. Thomas Jefferson warned, we are to be ruined by paper, as we were formerly by the old Continental paper. Two years later, he asserted that we are under a bank bubble that would soon burst. William Jones did not take steps to regulate the nation's currency, doled out huge loans that fed speculation and inflation. He also kept lax watch over state banks, where fraud and embezzlement created this chaos.

                            FAMILY
What do we do Pa? Davy Crockett said the whole banking system as nothing more than a species of swindling on a large scale.

                          WILLIAM CALL
There are two sets of rules. One for the elite and one for everyone else. So we have to create our own.

                            FAMILY
Give a man a gun, and he can rob a bank. Give a man a bank, and he can rob the world.

                           WILLIAM
Farmers rule, whoever owns the food makes the gold rulers starve. Leveling the field. A mans word is his bond. We will stay on this farm, regardless.

                            FAMILY
Ya Pa don't let them in. What about CLAY PEABODY Pa?
                           WILLIAM
                   (Looks down in anger.)

He, I guess will feed the rich, and we will feed the poor.

FADE OUT
INT. DAY - MATTS HOTEL ROOM

                              CHRISTINA BURZ
        (Laying naked in Matts bed as he returns from the store.)

Make love to me, for better or worse, bring fire to my fireplace, man
    of feeling, make love to me, make me warm. I want a child.

                              MATT HEMINGS
                               (Smiles.)

  Yes, beautiful, full of passion you are. Yes, let's be, as where a
  day shall feel like a week, and a week will be, of this love day.

  (Matt puts the do not knock sign on the door knob, closes the door,
                          and undresses.)

FADE OUT
INT. DAY - BANK

ASHER TOWN & MR. GREENWOOD were in the bank office.

                             MR. GREENWOOD
We won't have to worry, so let's see how they will rebound. Let's eat
    breakfast, and I will tell you how to be the eyes and ears on this
              investment. Spreading the American dream.

                              ASHER TOWN
  The power to tax is the power to destroy. Jackson will tell the
               people what they want to hear.

                              VIGILANTE
                        (Walked in the office.)

Do not make any fast stupid moves to protect yourselves. The farmers
  trusted you. I do not! How about this nightmare? I came to stop the
  bleeding. I am here at the source. I will be the one getting away
  with murder. You two are going to have to dance to this music I am
  playing. The name of the score is, taking out the trash, and when
      your head hits the floor the nation with sing the song.

  (Shoots them both in the throat, walks out the front door of the
          bank, gets on his horse and rides away.

          Two more fangs to go! The lower fangs!

(A bank teller crawls into a corner.)

FADE IN
INT. DAY - BLACKSMITH SHOP

                    BLACK SMITH FRANK LOCKWOOD
Bold and bloody it is. This has to be a a person that is a anti-
                            foreigner.

                         ELSY WHEELER
Or has faith in the sovereignty of the people. The U.S. Marshalls are
                            coming.

                    BLACK SMITH FRANK LOCKWOOD
They better bring lots of money. I own this shop. I do every job
   myself. I borrow nothing. I breed, and grow my own food.

                         ELSY WHEELER
You have character and reputation, and that's why I love you.

                    BLACK SMITH FRANK LOCKWOOD
The military enlistment numbers will go up.

                         ELSY WHEELER
The are turning this country into a card table.

                    BLACK SMITH FRANK LOCKWOOD
Hoard the gold, and put money in things that actually turn a decent
profit. Nothing good comes easy. Bartering, will always be the way to
go. I bet two hundred years plus from now, people will have to come
            back to this, and this eras wisdom.

                         ELSY WHEELER
I can't even fathom that Frank. I would rather help those who are
  struggling to improve themselves. What about the Judge Wood?

                    BLACK SMITH FRANK LOCKWOOD
He's so crooked, he could swallow nails and spit out corkscrews. You
          don't see him out here in this emergency.

FADE IN
INT. DAY - CHURCH

People gathered in, and outside of the Church. People born, and
raised in this Church, by blood and marriage.

                            PREACHER DUNN
                          Fear not the world!
                          (Read Genesis 34)

    Three days later, while all of them were still in pain, two of
Jacob's sons, Simeon and Levi, Dinah's brothers, took their swords
and attacked the unsuspecting city, killing every male. They put
Hamor and his son Shechem to the sword and took Dinah from Shechem's
house and left. The sons of Jacob came upon the dead bodies and
looted the city where their sister had been defiled. They seized
their flocks and herds and donkeys and everything else of theirs in
the city and out in the fields. They carried off all their wealth and
all their women and children, taking as plunder everything in the
                              houses.

The Coltsville 'Jailer and his family were there in prayer. The
Judge, and The Mayor were there, and their families too. Some people
in the pews stared at the mayor, in anger, why was he here, and not
out there controlling the chaos. The undertaker REX 'SPLINTER' WATERS
was there too, standing in the back, and the Jailer every once in a
while looked back at him. REX had more bodies to move, V.I.P. Bodies.

                            PREACHER DUNN
Then Jacob said to Simeon and Levi, You have brought trouble on me by
  making me obnoxious to the Canaanites and Perizzites, the people
  living in this land. We are few in number, and if they join forces
against me and attack me, I and my household will be destroyed. But
  they replied, Should he have treated our sister like a prostitute?

FADE OUT
EXT. DAY - BANK

Sheriff PAUL WALLACE, deputies, DR. ZANE SHULE, and the Newspaper man
stood outside the Bank.

                        SHERIFF PAUL WALLACE
    He likes to shoot them in the throat, and burn them alive.

                            DR. ZANE SHULE
                       He knows things we don't.

                        SHERIFF PAUL WALLACE
                       (Looks at the deputies.)

                            NEWSPAPER MAN
    Seventeen dead, what can I report to flush him out.

                    SHERIFF PAUL WALLACE
                  Maybe falsify an apprehension.

                 DR. ZANE SHULE & DR. SAPPINGTON
                    How would that stop this?

                    SHERIFF PAUL WALLACE
      The teller said, He said, two more fangs to go, the lower fangs.

                        NEWSPAPER MAN
              Interesting, he's calling his victims teeth.

                    SHERIFF PAUL WALLACE
      Report what happened, nothing else as of yet. I need info on all
      train arrivals, and departures. Locations from and to. Deputies, one
      of you to stand post there. Also one at the General store, and watch
                  for who seems suspicious making telegraphs.

FADE IN
NEXT DAY

POV
People of Coltsville read their morning paper.

                  The Vigilante Strikes in Daylight.
                  Three more dead, a total of seventeen.
                  The people of Coltsville need to be on watch
                        Vigilance is a crime!

INT. DAY - GENERAL STORE

MR. TEMPLE is reading the paper, as his son is facing, and stocking
the shelves.)

POV - Window shot
Outside the store CRAZY LESTER is gathering stones from the road, and
making stacks of rock piles.

                    SHERIFF PAUL WALLACE
                  (Comes into the store, and gets some coffee.)

Mr. Temple I need to know the correspondences of Mr. Applegate, Mr.
Fanning, Mr. Goldstien, and Mr. Rabenwitz. Most of all, put yourself
in my boots, and tell me something suspicious of folks that may
                    indicate who this Vigilante is.

MR. TEMPLE
This town is full of foul people, not many friendships. Fire and flame, and many hide knives under their pillows. Even me, and if you are looking to me to find the nature of a madman, then I suggest go to the theater play. King Lear is showing there. In my opinion this person is one of your companions.

PRAIRIE MARY DIVIN
(Was in the back having coffee, and walks and talks.)

There is a curse upon the land
Caused by a greedy, and unlawfulness hand
So who is it who spoils the hash?
Who declares themselves violent and rash?
What be the notion of a President?
Who all feels this carnage and element?
Who pays for this, tit for tat?
God knows, and thank God for that
God who sees all unguarded time
God who sees all un-moral crime
So who knows what is on each others mind?
Who is this violent temper of kind?
BYRON
(Applauded.)

The weight of this sad time we must obey. Speak what we feel, not what we must say. The oldest hathe born most. We that are young, shall never see so much, nor live so long.

SHERIFF PAUL WALLACE
At least here we know the press is not corrupt.

MR. TEMPLE
Not as yet. I do not read anything that would help you Sheriff, and if I do, I shall seek you. Also I can not lend a hand in the next election.

SHERIFF PAUL WALLACE
Election of what?
MR. TEMPLE
The presidency. I find it another curse upon this country. None are no Washington.

SHERIFF PAUL WALLACE
Thank you all for your time, and entertainment. Good Day.

(As the Sheriff walked out, a brief but stronger earthquake began,
              knocking things off of the shelves.)

                        SHERIFF PAUL WALLACE
(Looked at CRAZY LESTER, and back at the store, got on his horse, and
                            rode away.)

                           CRAZY LESTER
                   (Re-stacked his rock piles.)

FADE OUT
INT. NIGHT - OPERA HOUSE THEATER

Actors rearrange stage props from the earth shaking, and continue the
play.

MATT HEMINGS & CHRISTINA BURZ were in the theater laughing because
they enjoyed the shaking from the earthquake, and they began again
enjoying Shakespeares' King Lear, where the King divides the kingdom,
snubs daughter, goes mad, there's a storm, and everyone dies. They
sat there amazed, and felt too, the heart, and motivations of
Cordelia, and too disgusted by the power of greed.

MATT HEMINGS kisses CHRISTRINA.

FADE OUT
EXT. DUSK
POV- DRONE
The stretch from the bank where the bodies of MR.GREENWOOD & ASHER
TOWN are to the Church Cemetery is about a mile.

FADE IN

                       REX 'SPLINTER' WATERS
(Took the back road to the cemetery, and the ground shifted some from
   the earthquake, and without notice Rex moved forward, and once the
    back of the wagon rode over the deep rut, one of the back wheels
 broke. Slightly angry, Rex slowed down the horses, and wagon. He got
                off the wagon to observe the damage.)

      For heaven's sake, I need my men. Grrr Bristol wheels.
  (Rex kicks the broken wheel. He removed a horse from a harness, and
   rode to the cemetery where his men were digging graves for the two
                bodies in the back of the wagon.)

FADE OUT
EXT- DUSK - CHURCH CEMETERY
Two of Rexs undertakers are digging graves.

                              VIGILANTE
(Rode his horse to where they were, and got off. He slid his sword
slowly through his black gloved fingers, and walked towards the two.
   The two grave diggers, looked at each other, and fisted up their
                               shovels.)

FADE BACK IN
EXT- DUSK - BACK ROAD
                        REX 'SPLINTER' WATERS
                (Making the turn closer to the cemetery.)

FADE IN
INT - DUSK - TRAIN
The Train from Washington D.C. To Chicago. Two United States
Marshalls, and reporter from The National Intelligencer rode the
train to Coltsville.

   MARSHALL SKINNER, a tall, short blonde haired man with a trimmed
    thick mustache, once seen one could tell he was a man whom only
   resorted to violence when it was absolutely essential, but to be
           deadly efficient in its use as a last resort.

                          MARSHALL SKINNER
   Illinois should not be in the banking business. They mismanage
                            everything.

MARSHALL McDOWELL, a short stocky man, medium length dark haired man,
   with a goat-tee, once seen you could tell he was a worker, maybe a
   forty-niner, and seemed fearless, as though he has been shot a time
                            or two.

                          MARSHALL McDOWELL
                        Private banks too.

                    SAMUEL SEATON, a bright feller,
   I am writing a book on Vigilantes of our time. This one is a lone
                         wolf it seems.

                          MARSHALL SKINNER
           We can not trust anyone in Coltsville. Even the
well-respected and active in the affairs of their local community and
                              state.

                          MARSHALL McDOWELL
Only get information from a woman named ELSY WHEELER & FRANK LOCKWOOD
        We should be there on time in the morning.

FADE OUT
EXT. DUSK - CHURCH CEMETERY

The VIGILANTE and the two Gravediggers battle. REX 'SPLINTER' WATERS
sees them, and rides faster to the confrontation.

FADE IN
EXT. DUSK - TOWN SQUARE
The town is preparing for the nightlight celebration. The sun is
going down quick. People gather everywhere on both sides of the road
on main street for this extravaganza.

EXT. DUSK - CHURCH CEMETERY

CRAZY LESTER is watching this from afar, jumping up, and down
laughing.

The Vigilante toys with the Gravediggers. One gives away that REX is
coming closer from behind, so the VIGILANTE pulls out his long gun,
and shoots them both in the throat, and he runs to his horse, gets
on, and charges at REX.

REX slows down, pulls out a gun. The Vigilante diverts through the
cemetery in the direction of the Church, and REX follows.

FADE IN
EXT. NIGHT - CHURCH
                        THE PREACHER
     (Walking to the town square, and sees the Vigilante, and Rex in
                          pursuit.)

                        THE VIGILANTE
 (Riding fast right to town square, and the night is getting darker.)

                        THE PREACHER
     (Runs back into the Church, racing to ring the Bells.)

                    REX 'SPLINTER' WATERS
        (Gaining ground, closer he gets to the Vigilante.)

                        THE ELECTRICIAN
     (Puts his hands on the street lights power level.)

                        THE PREACHER
              (Gets his hands on the rope.)

THE VIGILANTE
(Turns on Main Street, and rides through the middle of the rode with his sword in hand, and long gun in the other.)

MR. TEMPLE & BYRON see the Vigilante first coming, then MATT & CHRISTRINA, REX comes around the corner in fast pursuit.

THE PREACHER rings the Church bells, at the same time THE ELECTRICIAN turns on the street lights. Everyone now sees THE VIGILANTE and REX riding right in front of them.

THE VIGILANTE
(Stops his horse, and turns it into the direction of REX. He lifts up his long gun, and goes into sniper mode in front of the whole town, and fires three shots into REX. Rex has no time, but to fall back off his horse, and into the dirt road.)

THE SHERIFF, and deputies glimpse the end of this, and run to their horses at the back of the jail. The Vigilante rides closer to REX, and shoots him two more times, and rides way. The Church bells stop, and the town is in awe. The gossip begins to bite everywhere in Coltsville, and many are in awe of the new streets lights.

CRAZY LESTER is in front of the Church jumping up, and down laughing.

The PREACHER keeps ringing the church bells. The Lawmen, ride away looking for the VIGILANTE.

ELSY WHEELER, FRANK LOCKWOOD & PRAIRIE MARY DIVIN look at each other, and smile.

CHRISTINA BURZ

Look MATT, on one side of the road are the CLAY PEABODYS farming family, and the other are the WILLIAM CALL farmer family. They all observed, and they all stare at one another. A showdown all its own, although they make the towns world show up.

FADE OUT
EXT. DAY – TRAIN STATION

Newspaper boy hustling newspapers. A deputy of the law sits on his horse watching people come to the station. Smoke of the steam train was seen from afar first, the ground shaking next.

PAPER BOY smiles, and looks at the ground, and smiles. The trains horn heard next as it slows down to stop at the station.

Newspaper reads 18 Dead, and Coltsville is a a Witness. Reward
$10,000.00 for the Vigilante.

MARSHALLS SKINNER & McDOWELL, and REPORTER SAMUEL SEATON un-board the
train, and FRANK LOCKWOOD, ELSY WHEELER, & PRAIRIE MARY DIVIN met
them there with three horses. The Coltsville deputy witnessed this,
and rode away to inform the Sheriff.

                          SAMUEL SEATON
             Paper boy I will take three, and pay for five.

                            PAPERBOY
                     WOW, thank you Mister.

                          ELSY WHEELER
               Gentlemen, I am Elsy Wheeler.

                         MARSHALL SKINNER
             Miss Wheeler can we go somewhere private?

                          FRANK LOCKWOOD
         Best to go to my shop. I have horses for you men.

                          ELSY WHEELER
                     Yes, there is good.

     (All six got on horses, and rode away to the Lockwood shop.)

FADE IN
EXT. DAY - HOSPITAL

DR. ZANE SHULE & DR. PIERRE SAPPINGTON, and all of the construction
workers were having a meeting, and Sheriff PAUL WALLACE rides up to
them.

                          DR. ZANE SHULE
The workers agreed to finish without Asher Towns so this is the good
news, but the bad news is, we have a flu epidemic in town too, and we
                  have no where to place people.

                       SHERIFF PAUL WALLACE
  It was only days ago when the Doctor of this town went to peoples
homes, and didn't this town hire your person here, Mr. Sappington?

DR. ZANE SHULE
Yes.

The deputy from the train station rode up.

DEPUTY
Two U.S. Marshalls and another man came in town today by train. The
train came from Washington D.C.

SHERIFF PAUL WALLACE
(Looks at everyone, chews his tobacco, and spits on the ground.)

DR. PIERRE SAPPINGTON
I will take the house work, you Dr. Shule take care of the bodies,
and the work here.

SHERIFF PAUL WALLACE
There are Electricians in town, get them a working here with us.

FADE OUT
INT. DAY - ON A COLTSVILLE FIELD - PICNIC
MATT HEMINGS
Writing is such a painful life, lonely, and well I can not avoid it
if I wish to. I enjoy it, it's a calling, but yes, it has turned out
that way, although I believe it be peaceful, and worth it. Actually
it amazes me, and reading does more to that as well.

CHRISTINA BURZ
(Snuggles up to MATT on the blanket as he thumbs through pages of his
writing.)

You should write about this town, and all this happening.

MATT HEMINGS
Yes beautiful.

FADE IN
INT. DAY - LOCKWOOD BLACKSMITH SHOP
PRAIRIE MARY DIVIN
Yesterday narrows suspects down.

ELSY WHEELER
Mr. Seaton, and Marshalls
I had to message you all because this town could be givin up as dead.
Even though death can all that happen to us. Maybe this shock is good
for us? We need noble businessmen, and lawmen here. I can not believe
all of this evil.

I was born the most trusting little person you ever saw. I was so
naive it's going to take me long to get on to what was going on here.
This senseless faith I have in life and in people, humanity, anything
what are the things, terrible things and yet not terrible, when I
consider what I know has happened to so many other people and even
people I know. My friends, these farmers. Members of my family, they
have it worse. I suffer from what is the sense of betrayal of my
belief being betrayed. We all here in Coltsville have been betrayed.
I do not want to harden my soul.

(Began to cry.)

We are good and evil and there is such a thing they're real and the
activeness. Our whole life is a challenge to us which way which we
will choose because we can't choose a challenging and what do not be
as evil as they are. I have enough evidence.

(Wipes her eyes.)

Look what's happening to our country and it cannot be destroyed
before it begins.

MARSHALL McDOWELL
We are not going to let it be destroyed. We are going to lose a great
deal but we're losing it now but you know this is the beginning of a
millennium and the end of an old one and there are new things even
the last ten years I have observed in just the human beings I know
and people that I have known. Like you Miss Wheeler.

MARSHALL SKINNER
A good attitude toward everything in life is key and there are some
new things coming I know you two see them. The world is not going to
end with either a bang or a whimper.

SAMUEL SEATON
Seems to this Mayor has to go also, and you Miss Wheeler should run
for Mayor after the Marshalls clean this town up.
FRANK LOCKWOOD
I would love that. Elsy would make a great Mayor of Coltsville.

PRAIRIE MARY DIVIN
Yes, I see it in the stars.

FRANK LOCKWOOD
Maybe we need two Sheriffs in Coltsville.

(The Marshalls look at each other.)

FADE IN
INT. DAY - SHERIFFS OFFICE
The mail man came in, and handed the Sheriff a letter, and left.

                          The letter read.
                               V.O.

Sheriff, I am asking you to turn yourself in for many things you have
done in this town, or pay the consequences.
  Siged, **V**

The Sheriff crumbles it up, and looks out the window.

FADE OUT
INT. DAY - GENERAL STORE

Mr. Temple and farmers Mr. Call & Mr. Peabody engage in business
talk.

                           MR. TEMPLE
               I know you both need a fair return.

                 CLAY PEABODY, a double crosser,
    I am not a hobby farmer like Mr. Call. I can not afford to take a
           loss. I have been fending for a fair return.

                (Mr. Calls blood began to boil.)

                           MR. TEMPLE
       The both of you have convictions to the town and the Nations
         prosperity's being bought at the both of your expense.

                          WILLIAM CALL
    I have been fighting the cost-price squeeze, and our capita has been
             shrinking, unlike this pampered tyrant.

                           MR. TEMPLE
        The both of you are primary producers of wealth.

                          WILLIAM CALL
  There is no balance with supply and demand here with you Mr. Temple.
    I have more overflow, so I will have to take it somewhere else.

                          CLAY PEABODY
                         Send it abroad.

                         WILLIAM CALL
        Are you ready to fight, like I do for my farm and family.

                         CLAY PEABODY
             I will turn you into peanuts Mr. Call.

                         MR. TEMPLE
     Alright, alight, listen, the both of you are bona-fide farmers here
                          in Coltsville.

                         WILLIAM CALL
      We will not need no bailout. Even so Congress, that let's it all run
                          on and on.

                         CLAY PEABODY
           Do you want to sell your farm to me Mr. Call.

                         WILLIAM CALL
           I had more than enough of your mouth.

      (Punches Mr. Peabody in the mouth, and Mr. Temple steps in to stop
        anymore scrapping. Clay spits out a tooth, and blood.)

                         BYRON
           (Looks at his father, and everyone in the store.)

FADE OUT
INT. NIGHT - CHURCH - WAKE

MRS. GREENWOOD, lawmen, and jailer, some town folk and a cousin of
REX were the only people there.

        THE PREACHER and his sermon for the Vigilante victims.
      My Brethren, with Christ by grace we are saved. Not by works of
    righteousness, which we have done, but according to his mercy we are
      saved, by the washing of regeneration, and the renewing of the Holy
                          Ghost.
The Coltsville Newspaper man was there writing obituaries.

FADE OUT
EXT. NIGHT- TALLEST HILL LOOKING OVER COLTSVILLE

                     SHERIFF PAUL WALLACE
                    (With his two deputies.)

                 One of you are the Vigilante.

They both look at each other, say not word, and not flinch.

The horses they ride stand still, until (POV)on that horse that grins... And the horses know what shall be.

FADE IN
EXT. FORTUNE TELLERS HOME

                        PRAIRIE MARIE DIVIN
   The dead are investigating themselves! See if your life line be a
                              future!

And the autumn winds began to blow in Coltsville, and CRAZY LESTER jumped up, and down!

FADE IN
INT. DAY - LOCKWOOD BLACKSMITH SHOP

                            ELSY WHEELER
This person may feel he is against this town, and the world itself.
 He believes his actions are protecting Coltsville, but so far, and
     good so far, this may not lead innocents getting hurt.

                           FRANK LOCKWOOD
   The people of this town needs to stop promoting an us vs. them
                             mentality.

                            ELSY WHEELER
  The social contract is so strong here. No one cares about, no one
 takes the problem seriously, and then it works its way up the social
                              scale.

      Everyone is going to have to see their own fears.

                           SAMUEL SEATON
I am worried all of this will cause people to act irrationally. We as
the republic are to be governed by reason and is therefore and all of
  this may stir up emotions on behalf of those who suffer and who
   therefore, potentially, can prompt people to act emotionally and
                            irrationally.

                           FRANK LOCKWOOD
A new legislation, allows a person to claim self defense if you shoot
              someone you feel threatened by.

                            ELSY WHEELER
      So we need to call for a town meeting about grief?

SAMUEL SEATON
Yes.

FRANK LOCKWOOD
Crying for ourselves rather for than the sufferer, blinds us to the
causes of human suffering, keeps us from doing anything useful about
preventing further occasions.

ELSY WHEELER
To bring out our best selves. Coltsville is our home.

EXT. DAY - RAILROAD

A mile north of the train station. A train derailed carrying gun
powder, and it exploded. The ground quaked, and the waters of the
Coltsville Bear River trembled. The wooden cars crumbled. People
covered in blood walked around in shock. WILLIAM CALL heard this from
his farm, and got on his wagon to help out on the scene. Bodies were
burned beyond recognition from the steam of the bursting boilers, and
gun powder bursts, many were crushed, dismembered and mutilated.
People of Coltsville stopped what they were doing, and ran toward the
sound. Bootleggers brought booze to comfort those who needed a drink.
Many came to help, but many came to gawk. The Pioneer Hook and Ladder
Fire Department came.

Sheriff & Deputies, and Coltsville newspaper mans' horses strode to
the scene of the disaster as the US Marshalls, and D.C. Newspaper man
stride to the scene also, and they see each other. The Power of the
Marshalls moved onto to them to engage their power.

MARSHALL SKINNER
Sheriff Paul Wallace you have fine ol' ugly mess on your hands here
in Coltsville, along with this here massive fire, and we want to know
how you and the Mayor are going to handle this, furthermore do not
say a word until I say speak.

We are U.S. Marshalls. Also the Mayor will be dealt with soon,
because our information leads to his cowardliness, and incompetence.
Seasons of this it seems. The luring scent of greed brings the scent
of blood, leading to the scent of a jail cell.

MARSHALL McDOWELL
No exports and imports from and to Coltsville is going to shut this
town down for a while, and you and your men, will, and must help find
people to bury these bodies here, and all. Was the derailment caused
by the Vigilante or Indians?

WILLIAM CALL and PREACHER DUNN came upon them.

                          MARSHALL McDOWELL
I know the Train Station has its own telegraph, and we must use it.

PREACHER DUNN spoke a prayer, and vomited from all the casualties
seen along the railroad tracks.

SAMUEL SEATON and Coltsville Newspaper man meet, shake hands, and
walk along the tracks talking to each other.

FADE OUT
EXT. DAY - COLTSVILLE ROAD

These three ladies walking to the railroad tracks.

                            ELSY WHEELER
I can tell you are a caring person Mrs. Greenwood. Unlike the evil
 people who run this town. I won't let their bad deeds reflect upon
you. Their career is to make this town safe, and prosperous, and they
 do not, they are brutal. I am angry but I won't let this town become
        a horrible place, and I feel that you feel the same way.

                          MRS. GREENWOOD
(Listens and tears fall from her eyes as they get closer.)

                        PRAIRIE MARY DIVIN
             The dead are investigating themselves.

                          MRS. GREENWOOD
(Sobs more, in account of her dead corrupted husband.)

                        PRAIRIE MARY DIVIN
We are upon an age of those who will give all, and receive little.

                          MRS. GREENWOOD
           I don't want to go crazy over this.

                           ELSY WHEELER
                   Join us in being defiant!

                        PRAIRIE MARY DIVIN
Yes join us, this is going to be action fun. We will gather the
                            cards.

ELSY WHEELER
We will stand our ground. We are first, and will be an example this town shall have. We are willing to pay the price, and make those responsible for this to pay more.

PRAIRIE MARY DIVIN
Our testimony in the west ceremony!

FADE IN
EXT. DAY - PEARL HOTEL

MATT HEMINGS
We must go to the train station too. I figured out who the Vigilante be, and I do not blame this spree. I am not going to tell you or anyone but write about him. God made it clear, I was born to write.

CHRISTINA BURZ
Do you love this country?

MATT HEMINGS
A patriot in the truest sense. History is stained with blood, and will be. The idea of America is a beautiful thing. I have love of mankind, and the joy of creation.

CHRISTINA BURZ
This town praises this person, a hero, so you think it's a man. They will pay for his defense if caught.

MATT HEMINGS
The mayor here is a joke, right?

CHRISTINA BURZ
(Laughs.)

MATT HEMINGS
It be fair play, and I believe it is not revenge, or prejudice.

CHRISTINA BURZ
If you want something done right, you have to do it yourself.

MATT HEMINGS
(Laughs.)

Right, we will never get abducted, because we are good people.

CHRISTINA BURZ
Do think people in the future would pay money to come back in time,
to us?

MATT HEMINGS
(Laughs loud.)

Yes! The pain and chaos channeling through my pen. God found a ray in
me, this moment to reflect the searing pain and sorrow in what people
do, and will do to each other on earth over money. The power of love
they will never know, it seems. Generations will be torn.

CHRISTINA BURZ
There is no such thing as anyone being ahead of their time, I
believe. We are a gift, and some have gifts, and a lot comes down to
respect for perspective. Seems you though Matt, clearly acknowledge
the divine source.

The wind came slowly, and strong, blowing the fires smoke through the
beautiful army of trees.

MATT HEMINGS
A new slavery to material things is being born.

A little ways back west on the Railroad Lester was stacking railroad
rocks, unwanted ones tossed to the sides, and sung.

CRAZY LESTER
Ever hear of Angela and John
It was two hundred years ago beyond
Angela was like David
John as Goliath
It happened in Virginia
She was the beginning of Hope
He was the an eclipse
Talking about deep rooted prejudice
And will never end
One of the other will be an extermination
And that's what other races want
People will not see this
But the outsiders looking in
Because this nation
Does not know how to master out sin
Something should have been handle before it begins

<pre>
                We are lucky to be alive
             And everyday will be a battle
              The abuse and use of good power
                To be enslaved like a beast
           And for centuries the shackles will rattle

                     Land Pyrates of
                   Negroes and Tobacco
                      Worse than hell
                   And new ways will come
                    And no one will tell

                    MATT & CHRISTINA
</pre>
Walked up quietly behind in the grass to LESTER, and they listened to
him without knowing.

AS LESTER RECITES HIS POEM, DEMONIC VERSIONS OF George Washington,
Ben Franklin, Abe Lincoln, Andrew Jackson, Ulysses Grant, Thomas
Jefferson and Alexander Hamilton, furthermore larger demons,
McKinley, Grover Cleveland, Salman Chase, James Madison, and Woodrow
Wilson stalk people of the U.S.A. Through different time warps, and
reveals these evil grins... And treacherous deeds.

<pre>
            Demons will be of this paper money
             It will reveal these demons faces
           This stuff will give people an evil glow
          And only love can tell, a false love will show
        A new history many will NOT be able to escape from
               Days of the new bloody sun

             These men are immortal evil spirits
                 Will control peoples minds
             By gamblers and preachers too blind
                  This will grow and grow
               And in many ways will grow
                Taking over peoples souls

             Money will be a tool over fools

                    The new weather
                  188$ all together
                  Demons skins leather
                      Add'em up!
                  I can see the Future
</pre>

MATT HEMINGS
(Applauds loudly, slightly startling Lester.)

Bravo, bravo Sir, you must be an Angel of sorts, I like that...

CHRISTINA
What are you a foot soldier for God?

LESTER
Yes I am mam.

MATT HEMINGS
I am a writer too. Let us walk into the other direction here on the railway tracks, and enjoy the beautiful world on both sides... Maybe we can find a place to swim.

LESTER
Yes, let's.

FADE OUT
EXT. DAY - COURTHOUSE

A riot began in Coltsville.

RIOTERS
(SHOUTING.)

$atan Lovers, $atan Lovers

Dirty men, dirty politics, dirty laws,
and these law men have soul flaws.
They say they are stuck in the middle,
The middle of what?
The rich and the poor
Our lives are not a poker table or craps

This is tearing up Gods given souls
Gods given lands
Gods given hands

We see the camouflage
You are killing this nation before it begins

FADE IN
INT. DAY - COURTHOUSE

JUDGE & MAYOR
(Peeking out the window, hearing the angry crowd.)

JUDGE
This reminds me of colonial Mexico. Cases I have learned in school.

THE VIGILANTE
(Walked into the room.)

No time for the rack, the whip, or a trial. Surrender to the people of Coltsville or die here by my hand. Be noble or lower class.

JUDGE
Your voice, I know it, but can not place it.

THE VIGILANTE
I bet you do, I know justifiable homicide more than you, and I am sick of you. I deserve praise because I find the worst scumpants alive, and kill them. The town is now behind me, so I will turn myself in if you all do, and your sick lawmen around here too. You have two minutes to decide.

MAYOR
I will surrender.

JUDGE
We can't.

THE VIGILANTE
Write a letter to your wives, and families, furthermore, write me a poem. Ode to the Vigilante.

(The Vigilante walks to the window, and the people of Coltsville see him, and stand in awe. He signals to be patient. The Judge and Mayor are disturbed as they try to write, they are deciding, thinking, and breaking down. He stands behind them with his gun pointing to the backs of their heads.)

FADE OUT
EXT. DAY - STREET OUTSIDE COURTHOUSE

Townsfolk conversing, inquisitive about what to do, and the actions the Vigilante be taking.

FADE IN
INT. DAY - COURTHOUSE

THE VIGILANTE
Need some help on that poem. Maybe like I failed at respect, duty and
impartiality in this black black robe. I am gutless like the banker
that is dead. The Coltsvilles Vigilante is wise, with no tolerance
eyes.

THE MAYOR
(Vomited.)

THE JUDGE
Just kill me, kill me.

THE MAYOR
Don't kill me, I have family. I will go out there, and face the town.

THE JUDGE
(Jumped on the Mayor, and began to punch him.)

THE VIGILANTE
My poem is about political control, lawmen control, and all sorts of
high crime criminals.

(Shouts out the window.)

The 18th Century is born EVIL! Grasp this, the ancient and the
modern. Congress drunk you are becoming. Congress drunk!

(Looked out the window, and motioned for the people to come in, come
up, and apprehend these two criminals. He waited a minute, walked
out, and slipped out of the courthouse.)

The People of Coltsville storm into the room. The Judge finds a gun,
shots the Mayor, and then himself before the people arrest them.

FADE OUT
EXT. DAY - WOODS

THE VIGILANTE
(In prayer.)

I am a tired watchman. A toiled man. Forgive me God. All of my
friends were friends until this new revolution, although I
understand. Bloody white picked fences. The worlds waywardness, and
now mine. Bummers upon bummers. I am trying to stop omens of the
future. I should have stayed a farm hand. Lord what am I to do about
the Rot-Gut Whiskey runners?

Deer, and Turkey roamed around him.

Our town is not civil or quiet. These people are like stray dogs, and
  hogs. Good families are declining, and I feel they will for a long
time. Good people feel they have no purpose, their good attitudes are
    dying, facts Lord. Sour, sour, sour. Things are bad, because of
  gutless leadership. This mess will never be fixed, it was designed
  and engineered on purpose by cruel and greedy men. I am trying for
the people, all people, and will die for it. I am trying to out smart
              them, because this system will exploit them.

God this government are like most, prone to violence. These newspaper
  men are next God, next to learn. I took out many of the feared King
  George troops to enslave the American Colonists in the days before,
and I will again. Fighting is the only solution for freedom. Nothing
  comes out of anything without losses or some sacrifices. Forgive me
                                God!

FADE OUT
EXT. DAY - ROAD TO COLTSVILLE

A Wells Fargo U.S. mail & Money wagon was riding into town, and a
Coltsville deputy stopped them, and spoke in secrecy.

FADE IN
INT. DAY - TRAIN STATION
MARSHALL SKINNER & McDOWELL watch Sheriff PAUL WALLACE, and his men
from the train station window.

                          MARSHALL McDOWELL
Are we going to apprehend them now, or use them for this disaster?

                          MARSHALL SKINNER
          (Turned around, and looked at Elsy & Frank.)

  Elsy I am going to deputize you as a U.S. Marshall, and you too
Frank. I imagine they won't go down easy. Train Station Master write
  down this message, and send it to Washington. Send a troop of the
Calvary here to Coltsville. The Paul Wallace law enforcement here are
engaged in all accusations. Surround the town, and send in men to me.
  We are going to engage now. We have no time to wait, this is a
                          priority case.

                          FRANK LOCKWOOD
                Elsy are you ready for this?

                          ELSY WHEELER
                         More than ever.

                        MARSHALL McDOWELL
We are going to lead them here, as to discuss these matters, and then
a go. It is for the Federal courts. We are the longer arm of the law.
    Raise your right hands, and I am going to swear you in.

              (Frank and Elsy were sworn in.)

Now this is one of the ropes you will learn. To apprehend Sheriff
Paul Wallace now before he becomes a fugitive. After this we are
       going to have to engage in all public safety roles.

                        MARSHALL SKINNER
     (Whistled for the Sheriff to come to the train station.)

         If he resists, we are going to take his life.

                          ELSY WHEELER
    Can I take off his tarnished badge, and spit in his face?

                (Skinner looked at McDowell.)

                        MARSHALL McDOWELL
        I can pass a Wheeler Act. It's a common defense.

Sheriff Paul Wallace tied a stick of dynamite to his backside
forearm, pulled his coat over it, and lit a cigar. He walked towards
the train station.

                        FRANK LOCKWOOD
Can I sharpen my ax? More commonly the skimmington ride, whereupon he
 to tie him backwards on a donkey, lead the beast through town facing
a shower of urine, excrement rotten fruit, and to take a beating with
                             sticks.

                        MARSHALL McDOWELL
             No. No violence, unless essential.

                        MARSHALL SKINNER
     He will be jailed, and taken to a Federal jail.

                          ELSY WHEELER
       He's coming, what is the amount of his award?

                    (They all laughed.)

                        FRANK LOCKWOOD
                We can't let his deputies get away.

The Marshalls looked at each other, and did not say a word.

                        FRANK LOCKWOOD

Me, and Elsy are wearing iron plates I've made under our clothes
                Marshalls, may God be with you.
                      MARSHALL SKINNER
                We have been in many true gun fights.

                    SHERIFF PAUL WALLACE
        (Walked in the train station, and looked at Elsy.)

        It's a great day to hunt, and it has to be men.

                      MARSHALL McDOWELL
                  Please have a seat Sheriff.

                    SHERIFF PAUL WALLACE
              Happy to, so what's on your mind?

The train station telegrapher walked out.

                      MARSHALL McDOWELL
      Decency, and honesty. Most of all failed attempts of Peace here in
                          Coltsville.

                    SHERIFF PAUL WALLACE
                          (Smirked.)

    The people here are immoral and parasitic. They have their own
supplies and demands. To detect and control this town one would have
to be a super sheriff. Like you, and your partner here. There are
many super villains here. Taxes are high Marshall, and so are the
stakes here in Coltsville. Shadow, shadows. You know baby-sitting
crime is high here too. There is a mandate from Heaven, and one from
            Hell. Maybe you do not like theocracy but I do.

                        ELSY WHEELER
        We must tax the rich, to help the working people and the poor.

                    SHERIFF PAUL WALLACE
Never doubt the ability of humans to deceive themselves, and others.

                          ELSY WHEELER
                    Railroad taxes, and axes.

                         FRANK LOCKWOOD
                       (Looking nervous.)

                      SHERIFF PAUL WALLACE
God's word already said this would happen. Then I saw another beast
  coming up out of the earth, and he had two horns like a lamb and
 spoke like a dragon. And he exercises all the authority of the first
beast in his presence, and causes the earth and those who dwell in it
   to worship the first beast, whose deadly wound was healed. He
 performs great signs, so that he even makes fire come down from
               heaven on the earth in the sight of men.

(The sheriffs hand was quicker than their eyes, but not their ears.
                     The fuse was lit.)

And he deceives those who dwell on the earth by those signs which he
was granted to do in the sight of the beast, telling those who dwell
 on the earth to make an image to the beast who was wounded by the
                       sword and lived.

         (The fuse fizzed shorter, and closer to blast.)

                         FRANK LOCKWOOD
    (Shot the sheriff in the head, ran towards Elsy, and the door.)

Elsy, and the Marshalls followed, and boom. The train station blew
up, and they all hit the ground.

FADE IN

EXT. DAY - COLTSVILLE WOODS

The Vigilante seen the station blow up from the woods.

                         THE VIGILANTE

                         He was mine.

                   (Rode away into the woods.)

FADE OUT

EXT. DAY - COLTSVILLE BEAR RIVER

                         MATT HEMINGS

  Do you think people care about the wisdom in the bible, like the
 Psalms, Proverbs, and various other valuable stories in the bible?

                        CRAZY LESTER
                    Seems people do not.

                      CHRISTINA BURZ
              When people feel rigid they retreat.

                       MATT HEMINGS
                  What makes people feel rigid?

                      CHRISTINA BURZ

Money is an extreme force that puts people into damning predicaments.

                        CRAZY LESTER

      As a society, it forces people to compete against each other.

                       MATT HEMINGS

Why can't we go back to notched twigs to feathers and construction
                  nails for debt or favor?

                  (Kisses Christina.)

We would need to move beyond the idea of exchange altogether. We need
to imagine a world of equal access. A world where we all have access
to healthcare, housing, and food, and even everything we consider
leisure, advancement, entertainment and new wagons, and more
importantly it would be a world that doesn't require anything in
exchange for them, a world where all of this, is free.

                (Kisses Christina again.)

We all depend on each other and that we exist in a society that
depends on us pitching in, and pushing it forward. All we need are
things that hold social utility the things that are necessary for
survival and that make life worth living. We need to be looking for
ways to develop ourselves and society.

                        CRAZY LESTER

Resources fuel fear, the lack of. These lands and its natives, can
feed the whole world. Talking about a common ownership, and democracy
to where those resources should go and how.

                       MATT HEMINGS

We deserve to see ourselves as something more. To see ourselves in a
world where we can be unleashed and empowered to give into society
based on our natural abilities and take from it based on our needs?

CHRISTINA BURZ

We must teach our youth the beautiful ways of the world.

We must do, and not dream. A world driven by passion & love instead of survival and fear. I truly believe that if all families needs are met, they would be so much more involved with society and would go above and beyond with helping fellow man kind. We all would truly have a better, different life that would be healthier than now, and the future.

FADE IN

EXT. DAY - GENERAL STORE

WILLIAM CALL called a town meeting before ELSY WHEELER.

WILLIAM CALL

Somethings do not change over time, and some people make sure this does not happen. I have no flimsy evidence. I see America as a permanently divided country. It is the new rule in American life, not the exception, this be authentically American, the new American thinking.

We have to fight our way, as farmers. Real estate is a new manipulation upon this nation. This is not a myth, and beginning of a long long nightmare. We must love one another not lust one another. A true noble blood, and country and we must love the natives, and blend our agriculture wisdom, because they can teach us more than we can know, ever!

We must harvest a generation of wisdom, and wisdom people. Farmers we must continue to plow our fields with love and lovers must continue to flirt with love. Love only, through true loving wisdom. Our horses, we must love our horses. We can not get sucked into this evil. That will keep you in constant misery. Beware of the cities upon the hills. Hod butchers upon the world. We must be the plow, and the reaping machine. We must learn crop rotation, and not kill the harvest, our food, and people along with their souls. We must also watch the railroads, and become regulators. We must co-op. A farmers alliance, and a wisdom alliance. We the common man and farmer are important. Our stories must not die. Everyone, all of us prosper. We can not let our history repeat itself, never. Thou shalt not crucify mankind on a cross of MONEY!

We must keep our pioneering optimism, march on Washington, free ourselves from the banks, free ourselves from this enslavement, and pressure politicians to endorse us all, and return to prosperity. To do so, we must live up to our potential, all of us farmers using our brains, all workers discovering their hearts, and leaders displaying courage.

We must also love literature! This will lift the shadows that hang over us, and also write anew. We must honor the call within our self and follows it.

Preacher Dunn, you must also learn other hearts of literature. It will enlarge your heart.

Sadly, we have bodies to bury at the train station. We must do this together. Winter is upon us, we must prepare for that together.

ELSY WHEELER
(Applauded)

William Call for mayor of Coltsville. I am your new Sheriff, sworn in by the Unites States Marshalls. Elizabeth Greenwood is here to take over the bank, and speak to you all one on one, until everyone's concerns are heard. Mr. Frank Lockwood is here to take care of your teeth. Our towns Doctors Dr. Shule and Sappintington are here too to help you all.
CLAY PEABODY
You still have problem on your hands, me.

FRANK LOCKWOOD
Simmer down Mr. Peabody, you are not all that high and mighty!

The Crowd applauded, and the newspaper men took this to all national news, real news the nation needed to know.

ELSY WHEELER
Let us all help Mr. Clay, and Preacher Dunn with the victims of the train explosion.

FADE OUT
EXT - DAY - BEAR RIVER

MATT HEMINGS
We must, all of this nation must protest all sorts of heartbreak. Words, and standing by them are the poor mans weapons. Always has been, and always will.

                          CHRISTINA BURZ
I can see the future if not, meaning the people of the future will
                   have gun control issues.

                          CRAZY LESTER
Along with vocabulary issues, as in reading and writing, in full,
understanding by listening too, the arts of all arts, in hearts!

                          MATT HEMINGS
Right. Writing and imagination are divine like, period. Individuality
  be windividuality. As in when I can get Christina to stay in one
   place. I love looking at her cheeks, because I can see her true
     beautiful being, her spirit. Look, look at her essence.

                          CRAZY LESTER
                         Empathy issues.

                          CHRISTINA BURZ
                  (Shows Matt loving affection.)

Two Shawnee warriors rode up to them in a canoe.

          SHAWNEE 1 RED MOON, a tall man with a Mohawk.
We seek no harm, and do no harm, and require no government. All life
  is native, comes from mother earth and return's to her. Do no harm
  spirits travel the universe. We know how to operate outside of the
               evil corporate roman death cult government.

                          MATT HEMINGS
  I love and respect your strong connection to each other and your
honored Ancestors, and also your great knowledge of plants and trees
            for medicinal healing purposes and much more.

It makes me sick what's being done to Native Americans, and Negroes
by European so-called settlers and by the current extremely corrupt
  government. Yes I am white, but I know what be wrong and right.

        SHAWNEE 2 BLACK HOOF, tall and stocky, with long hair.
                      This invade will fade.

                          CHRISTINA BURZ
In many moons from now yes, an at large snarge, a large snarge.

                           RED MOON
Let us all sit, and go on a vision quest. Sing sacred songs, and see
                   things coming from above.

BLACK HOOF
We connect with another of higher dimensions. Intimacy with energy,
realizing that time is a restraint, that our spirit is trapped inside
our body. We pray, and we are used to performing what others say are
miracles. Healing people, and we know that we belong outside of this
world, time, and space.

RED MOON & BLACK HOOF tied up their canoe, got out, shook hands, and
put two feathers in Matts, Christina, and Lesters hair, and pointed
up. They smoked from a peace pipe, and between them were peace. They
spoke wisdom to each other, recited poems, and laughed, having a good
time while long hunters and frontier traders spied on them.

RED MOON
I am Red Moon, Mškwaawi Tepekikiišθwa, and this is Black Hoof. We are
brothers.

MATT HEMINGS
Nice to meet you two. Christina, Lester, and I am Matt.
I don't like liars, and thieves. I am sure you all do not either.

CHRISTINA BURZ
I wonder what they are doing in town?

MATT HEMINGS
Sodom and Gomorrah.

CRAZY LESTER
You know how white people are, all about blood and revolutions.
Alcohol anarchy effects everyone.

CHRISTINA BURZ
A cause whereby those who act do so knowing they are perpetrating the
same actions that caused it, it almost seems like some sort of
prolonged mass hysteria... I drink, so I understand.

MATT HEMINGS
The Constitution be brilliant though. I believe peaceful revolutions
can be successful without massive civilian casualties.

RED MOON
(Packed the pipe again, and passed it to them.)
Big Knives. Seek. Rugh, nekana.

MATT HEMINGS
This country be great and all we need. Like Christina, she is all I
need. Love be an overdraft.

BLACK HOOF
We are suppose to walk around these trees, whistle in one breath.

RED MOON
No evil spirits live in these Yeandawa waters.

BLACK HOOF
The Great Spirit alive, Wishemenetoo.

RED MOON
(Laid back on the grass.)
Ake.

CHRISTINA BURZ
So let us speak, and blend the arts of life.

BLACK HOOF
Our people too came from across the sea. We must not fail at
agriculture, and set up a station with you, and not Coltsville. This
will stop uncertainty. We have warned colonial officials.

MATT HEMINGS
It's all divide and conquer, the devils tongue.

(He carved his initials in a tree. M.H.)

CRAZY LESTER
I can return to Africa now, law provides. I just need to find an
appointed agent.

As the hunters watched them, one pointed his rifle at them.

BLACK HOOF
You should stay, and help us with the fish trade.

CHRISTINA BURZ
Don't you work at the saw mill?

CRAZY LESTER
One day a week, and they are starting a shingle factory.

MATT HEMINGS
We should stay right here, and build tree houses, and live from the
river.

CHRISTINA BURZ
People will sadly chop this forest away.

Another hunter pointed his rifle at them.

                         MATT HEMINGS
Money and war will keep people as animal like, and not human. This
             country is broke. In debt from war.

                          CHRISTINA
      The Government should mind to its own affairs.

The Vigilante came upon the wilderness men, and shot the men with the
rifles in the back of the head. Scaring Matt and company.

                         VIGILANTE
      Negro hunting now is illegal, and I am on Patrol.

              (Shots the other men in the throat.)

                         RED MOON
                   We are being ambushed.

      (He, and Black Hoof reach for their bow and arrows.)
                         MATT HEMINGS
                No, that be the Vigilante.

The Vigilante raised both of his arms to Matt and company, as a V,
meaning Victory.

                         MATT HEMINGS
                          (Whistled.)

      Come down here, and join us. We would love to meet you.

The Vigilante stood there for a moment and walked away.

FADE OUT
INT. DAY - LOCKWOOD BLACKSMITH SHOP

Prairie Mary Divin and the Lytton Boy were bathing horses.

                         LYTTON BOY
                   (Lathering a horse.)

          My Mothers horse drowned in the river.

                          PRAIRIE MARY DIVIN
                          (Rinsing same horse.)

                    Oh my. Was she riding the horse?

                              LYTTON BOY
No. Last years rains and flood. A mob of town folk tried to save him,
  but it was to late. Mother said, he panicked, lost its footing and
                         possibly broken a leg.

                          PRAIRIE MARY DIVIN
                          Sorry to hear this.

                              LYTTON BOY
                              (Smiles.)

            I think these Marshalls are all show.

                          PRAIRIE MARY DIVIN
                          (Laughed.)

                    You may have a point.

A six-horse wagon came thundering to the shop. It was full of fur.
                              MAN
   Howdy, we need new shoes for each horse. We came from the Rockies.

                              LYTTON BOY
                    I will go get Mr Lockwood.

                    (Ran out into town.)

                              MAN
                They too can use a wash. How much?

                          PRAIRIE MARY DIVIN
                          We only take gold.

                              MAN
Who wouldn't? All this money crap for the birds.

                          PRAIRIE MARY DIVIN
                    Help me with the horses Sir.

                              MAN
                          Yes, mam.

FADE IN
EXT. DAY - TEMPLE GENERAL STORE

The LYTTON BOY ran to the store looking for Frank Lockwood, and seen
the Electrician, working in the new hospital. He seen Dr. Shule and
Dr. Sappington, and the LYTTON BOY ran along side the U.S. Calvary
that came into town with U.S. Mail & Money wagon, and the Marshalls
and Sheriff Elsy Wheeler met them at the store.

FADE IN
INT. DAY - TEMPLE GENERAL STORE

                         SAMUEL SEATON
                          (Writing.)

I am staying in Coltsville, you need another newspaper here in this
                    turbulent time of politics.

                    COLTSVILLE NEWSPAPER MAN
                How would this help the both of us?

                         SAMUEL SEATON
    The population is exceeded 50,000. We could boast each other, and
  conflict each other to gain subscribers and compete in advertising,
                but share printing debts on machinery.
                    COLTSVILLE NEWSPAPER MAN
   This is a time of wild financial speculation, a hard crash, and I
                       feel another is coming.

                         SAMUEL SEATON
 Our reports are in an objective manner with the events of the world.
 You have been a faithful watchman for the people and the public good,
        and I can get your articles in Washington, and abroad.

                    COLTSVILLE NEWSPAPER MAN
    I agree, and every morning we should be in high spirits.

                         SAMUEL SEATON
          Oh come on, we can curse a little too.

                    COLTSVILLE NEWSPAPER MAN
                          (Laughed.)

                The Vigilante is still at large.

                        SAMUEL SEATON
              I confess, seems to be superior.

                   COLTSVILLE NEWSPAPER MAN
          Poetry is common here in Coltsville. Keats.

                        SAMUEL SEATON
    Agreed. Common as Vigilante shadows. Problems we will have are, the
          Marshalls, accountability, and prosecution.

                   COLTSVILLE NEWSPAPER MAN
    To me, I do not see a tree from which the Vigilante will hang from.
    The people here will smile now, and show their teeth in a non-jury
        way. They will share a memory loss, and I can put gold on it.

FADE OUT
INT. NIGHT - MATTS ROOM - PEARL HOTEL

                        MATT HEMINGS
      Beautiful Christina our love shall triumph. We shall glow, we are
    struck by love fire. We have forbidden charm defying all tyranny. You
            are poetry and me, prose, and together, we revolt.

                        CHRISTINA BURZ
                        I'll marry you.

    They made love, and went to sleep. Matt asleep although dreaming. The
    man upstairs be rude, and never takes off his cowboy boots. The man
    must be out of his mind.

POV
MAN UPSTAIRS
    Matt pictured him pacing to and fro bored, and not realizing his
    ignorance of noise. Matt aggravated from sleep loss, grabbed
    Christinas' gun, stood up, pointed the gun at the ceiling. He
    listened to and for the mans place, and once heard the man walk. Matt
    shot many rounds up through the ceiling. Matt awoke, listening to the
    man upstairs pace back, and force. Matt got up, looked at Christina
    in her beauty sleep, and he smiled. He went to the window, opened it,
    and the birds sang.

                        MATT HEMINGS
      Life be good. Thank you Great Spirit. Love strikes throughout the
                             earth.
                    (Yelled out the window.)

              Love thy neighbor.

FADE OUT
INT. DAY - COURTROOM

Widow Ms. Elizabeth Greenwood, and Sheriff Elsy Wheeler swore in the
Jailer to be the new Judge of Coltsville.

POV - FOURTH WALL

                          JAILER
                Do not befoul Coltsville!

FADE OUT
POV COLTSVILLE
small EARTHQUAKE

                        CRAZY LESTER
                (Stacking rocks by the railway.)

 History going to repeat and repeat and repeat. No one will learn to
                          listen.

                        THE END!

ya ya th'C inside th'Circle John E. WordSlinger

Poetry Train
http://www.poetrytrain.com

Amazon Author Page:
https://www.amazon.com/Mr-John-E-WordSlinger/e/B01AF3E55M

Blogs:
https://johnewordslinger.wordpress.com
https://speakofthepoetandthepoem.wordpress.com/